READY, SET, DRAW!

COOL GIRL STUFF
YOU CAN DRAW

Nicole Brecke

Patricia M. Stockland

M Millbrook Press / Minneapolis

The images in this book are used with the permission of: © iStockphoto.com/Dzianis Miraniuk, p. 4; © iStockphoto.com, pp. 4, 5, 7, 9, 22–23; © iStockphoto.com/Boris Yankov, p. 5; © iStockphoto.com/ JR Trice, p. 5; © iStockphoto.com/Brent Melton, p. 11; © iStockphoto.com/James Steidl, pp. 18–19; © iStockphoto.com/Randy Mayes, pp. 26-27; © iStockphoto.com/Vladimir Piskunov, pp. 30–31.

Front cover: © iStockphoto.com (forest); © iStockphoto.com/Brent Melton (flowers); © Michaela Stejskalova/Shuterstock Images (hand).

Edited by Mari Kesselring
Research by Emily Temple

Millbrook Press
A division of Lerner Publishing Group, Inc.
241 First Avenue North
Minneapolis, MN 55401 U.S.A.

Website address: www.lernerbooks.com

Library of Congress Cataloging-in-Publication Data

Brecke, Nicole.
    Cool girl stuff you can draw / by Nicole Brecke and Patricia M. Stockland ; illustrations by
Nicole Brecke.
        p.   cm. — (Ready, set, draw!)
    Includes index.
    ISBN: 978–0–7613–4164–2 (lib. bdg. : alk. paper)
    1. Drawing—Technique—Juvenile literature. I. Stockland, Patricia M. II. Title.
NC655.B75 2010
743—dc22   2009009933

Manufactured in the United States of America
1 2 3 4 5 6 – BP – 15 14 13 12 11 10

TABLE OF CONTENTS

ABOUT THIS BOOK

Unicorns, performers, and athletes! This gathering of girl stuff is just for you! With the help of this book, you can begin drawing your favorite things. Sketch a soccer player. Or create a castle. Soon you'll know how to draw many cool creations.

Follow these steps to create each character. Each drawing begins with a basic form. The form is made up of a line and a shape or two. These lines and shapes will help you make your drawing the correct size.

A First, read all the steps and look at the pictures. Then use a pencil to lightly draw the line and shapes shown in RED. You will erase these lines later.

B Next, draw the lines shown in BLUE.

C Keep going! Once you have completed a step, the color of the line changes to BLACK. Follow the BLUE line until you're done.

WHAT YOU WILL NEED

PENCIL SHARPENER

COLORED PENCILS

HELPFUL HINTS

Be creative. Use your imagination. Read about ballerinas, snowboarders, or castles. Then follow the steps to sketch your own book of cool things.

Practice drawing different lines and shapes. All your drawings will start with these.

Use very light pencil lines when you are drawing.

Helpful tips and hints will offer you good ideas on making the most of your sketch.

Colors are exciting. Try to use a variety of shades. This will add value, or depth, to your finished drawings.

Keep practicing, and have fun!

ERASER

PENCIL

PAPER

HOW TO DRAW A CASTLE

Many maidens have daydreamed of living in a castle. With a drawbridge, a moat, and a tower, what could be more romantic? Castles were actually fortresses as well as status symbols. The moat and tall, thick walls could protect the lords and ladies from enemies. And the tower's high view helped guardsmen keep watch in case of attacks. Inside the walls, a broad courtyard allowed peasants to sell their goods. And the royal families would reign over all inside the castle's gate. What does the castle in your kingdom look like?

1 Lightly draw a small base triangle and a center line. Add a base rectangle. Outline the triangle and the rectangle to make the roof and the front wall. Add two vertical lines to connect these shapes.

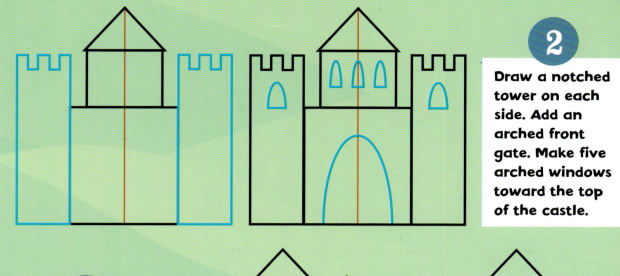

2

Draw a notched tower on each side. Add an arched front gate. Make five arched windows toward the top of the castle.

3

Carefully erase your center line. Add three pairs of horizontal lines to the gate.

4

Now it's time to color your castle!

7

HOW TO DRAW A UNICORN

Part horse. Part legend. The unicorn and its story are wrapped in mystery. This creature is often found in mythology (a collection of stories and beliefs). Tales about this magical white horse with a single horn have been told for more than two thousand years. Some myths claim that the unicorn is nearly impossible to catch. But if caught, a unicorn can bring many good things to its keeper. The mystical creature's horn is said to have healing powers. Have you ever seen a unicorn?

1 Draw a light base oval. Add a bent baseline. Make a larger base circle at the angled point. Add a slightly smaller base circle to the end of the baseline.

2 Draw the backbone by connecting the base oval and the circles. Make the ear, the forehead, the muzzle, the neck, and the front shoulder.

3 Add a long tail and a flowing mane. Use curvy vertical lines to draw the legs. Add hooves. Draw a slightly curved belly and a shorter curved line.

4 Carefully erase your baseline and shapes. Add an eye, a nostril, and a pointed horn.

5 Now it's time to color your unicorn!

HOW TO DRAW A FAIRY

Folklore includes many famous fairies, such as pixies, leprechauns, and Cinderella's fairy godmother. Fairies are creatures of magic and tricks. Legends describe these supernatural beings in many different ways. Most fairies are said to be tiny. They have wispy wings and are able to grant wishes. Fairies often carry wands, and they have the power to become invisible. In myths and stories, these little people often live in the meadows and woods. Those are perfect places to protect their fairy gold!

1 Lightly draw a small base circle and a baseline. Extend the baseline with an angled line. Add a face profile and a hairline to the circle.

2 Draw a shoulder, an arm, and a hand. Add a small dress. Make the other shoulder. Use a longer, curved shape to finish the other arm and hand.

3

Follow the baseline to draw the front leg and foot. Add the back leg and foot. Make a pair of wings.

4

Carefully erase your baselines. Draw a headband. Add an eyebrow, a closed eye, and a mouth.

5 Now it's time to color your fairy!

HOW TO DRAW A
BALLERINA

Dance is one of the oldest forms of entertainment. In the mid–1600s, dancers began to standardize ballet movements and skills. The beauty of ballet comes from many things. Technique, grace, costumes, and music are all important. But people also love ballet for its creativity. Ballerinas work with choreographers (people who create steps for dancers to follow). The dancers use different steps to show feelings, ideas, and actions. Whether dancing on pointe (tiptoe) or leaping into a grand jeté (full split), your ballerina can grace the stage with her talent.

1 Draw a small base circle. Add a curved baseline. Extend that baseline, and angle the end. Add another vertical baseline. Add a face and neck profile, a hairline, and a bun to the circle.

2 Use horizontal lines to draw an extended arm and hand. Add a chest line, a skirt, and an arched back. Make the other arm extended upward.

3

Draw the extended back leg with the foot pointing outward. Make a standing leg and another pointed toe.

Draw two
connecting
lines at the
shoulder for the
leotard strap.
Add two short
lines under
the skirt. Make
ribbon lines at
the ankles and
add a shoe line.

5 Carefully erase your base
shape and lines.

6 Add a small eye.
Make a U shape
for the ear.

TRY THIS
Use light pink to color the tights.

Giselle, *The Nutcracker*, and *Swan Lake* are all famous ballets.

HOW TO DRAW A
SINGING STAR

Rock, folk, classical, pop, rap, and jazz—almost everyone has a favorite type of music. Long ago, minstrels (singing poets) put their poems to music to make them easy to remember. In this way, certain pieces of music became popular. Modern songs still tell stories. But musicians now have many instruments with which to create music. Singers often back up their vocals with a guitar, a piano, or crashing drums. But the voice might still be the ultimate instrument. What type of music does your star sing?

1

Lightly draw a small base oval. Add a baseline. Make a large base triangle.

2

Make a U shape for the bottom of the face. Add a short wave of hair and a longer wave. Draw three jagged lines below this.

3

Draw an arm and hand reaching upward. Make the other arm bent in a V shape, and add a curved hand.

4

Follow the base triangle to make the dress. Add a curved chest line to connect the arms and the dress.

5

Carefully erase your baselines and shapes.

6

Use four thick, short horizontal lines for eyes and eyebrows. Make two small dots for nostrils. Add a mouth.

LOUD
AND PROUD

When singers want to get their voice into the crowd, they grab a microphone.

DRAW A MICROPHONE!

A

B

C

Jazz and blues music began in the United States.

7 Now it's time to color your singing star!

QUICK TIP

Add details to the dress to make it one of a kind.

HOW TO DRAW A SOCCER PLAYER

How fast can you run? How well can you kick? Soccer players control the ball with their sure skills and quick feet. Modern soccer began in the United Kingdom in the late 1800s. British soldiers brought the game to other nations, and it quickly caught on. In 1991, the Women's World Cup was created. Players such as Mia Hamm and Julie Foudy became soccer heroes! Whether dribbling down the field or doing some fancy footwork to get the ball beyond the goalie, you can have an amazing time playing soccer. What moves does your soccer player have?

1 Draw a light base oval, a center line, and two angled baselines.

2 Draw a hairline, a jawline, and an ear. Add the top of the head and a ponytail.

3 Make the collar, two short sleeves, and the bottom of the shirt. Use horizontal lines to make an arm and hand extending from each shirtsleeve.

4 Add shorts below the waistline. Draw legs extending from the shorts. Make socks on each leg. Add shoes below each sock.

5 Erase your baselines and shapes.

6 Add short, curved lines for eyebrows and eyes. Make a small U shape for the nose. Add a mouth.

KICK IT!

The hexagon and pentagon shapes on a soccer ball help hold it together during a turf battle.

DRAW A SOCCER BALL!

A

B

C

QUICK TIP
Mix colors to
add depth.

MORE PEOPLE in the world play
soccer than any other sport.

HOW TO DRAW A FIGURE SKATER

Modern figure skating combines strength and grace. But ice-skating began as a simple way to get somewhere faster! In the Netherlands, people on skates could use the frozen canals as slick, quick streets. Skating fast was also a fun winter pastime. During the late 1800s, American dancer Jackson Haines helped turn the hobby of winter skating into figure skating. He performed dance moves while ice-skating. People loved it. By the early 1900s, clubs for figure skaters formed. Have you ever dreamed of becoming a figure skater?

1 Draw a light base oval and a curved baseline. Add a short line and a face profile to the top of the oval. Add a hairline to the bottom of the oval. Finally, add a ponytail.

Draw a bent vertical line upward for the arm. Add a mitten. Draw two more vertical lines, a cuff, and a mitten to finish the other arm.

3 **Add a curved collar. Draw the front of the shirt, the waist, and the back of the shirt. Draw two pairs of lines, each connected with a short line, for the legs.**

4 **Add a boot to the bottom of the standing leg. Make a skate blade on the boot. Add another skate to the extended leg.**

6 Draw the eyebrow, the eye, and the mouth using short lines. Make a curved line for the ear.

GRAB YOUR GEAR

A skate bag helps a figure skater protect her blades and gear.

DRAW A SKATE BAG!

A

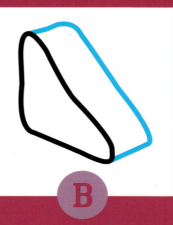

B

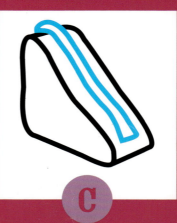

C

Olympic
figure skaters
can compete
in singles,
pairs, and
ice dancing
events.

7 Now it's time to color your figure skater!

HOW TO DRAW A SNOWBOARDER

Dashing through the snow on a board that cuts down the slopes—that's what snowboarding is all about! This sweet sport is as fun as the snow is cold. Snowboarding was invented by combining the sports of surfing and skiing. In the 1960s, the first real snowboard was built. A ski resort called the Suicide Six held a snowboard race in 1982. And by 1998, snowboarding had become popular enough to gain a spot in Olympic competition. Have your snowboarder race the slalom or do tricks on the half-pipe.

1 Lightly draw a base oval and a baseline. Extend the baseline with an angled line.

2 Outline the head, and add squiggly lines for hair.

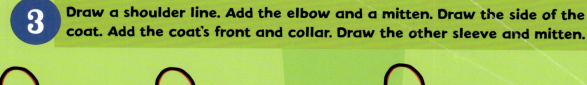

3 Draw a shoulder line. Add the elbow and a mitten. Draw the side of the coat. Add the coat's front and collar. Draw the other sleeve and mitten.

4 Make two parallel curved lines for the front leg. Draw a long oval for the snowboard. Add short lines for the back leg. Draw the boot tops.

Fast Fact...

THE FIRST SNOWBOARD, INVENTED IN THE 1960s, WAS CALLED A SNURFER.

5 Add a line over the shoulder that runs down the front of the coat and front leg.

6 Carefully erase your baselines.

SOME snowboarders compete in an obstacle course called snowboard cross.

7 Draw large goggles. Add short horizontal lines for the nose and the mouth.

8 **Now it's time to color your snowboarder!**

Professional snowboarders can do tricks such as ollies, alley oops, and grinds.

TRY THIS

Draw snow under the snowboard. Use light grays to shadow it.

FURTHER READING

Brecke, Nicole, and Patricia M. Stockland. *Horses You Can Draw*. Minneapolis: Millbrook Press, 2010.

Dubosque, Doug. *Draw 3-D: A Step-By-Step Guide to Perspective Drawing*. Columbus, NC: Peel Productions, 1998.

Girls Inc.
https://www.girlsinc-online.org

Grau, Andree. *Dance*. New York: DK, 2005.

King, Bart. *The Big Book of Girl Stuff*. Layton, UT: Gibbs Smith, 2006.

United States Olympic Committee. *Women in Olympic Sports*. Santa Ana, CA: Griffin Publishing Group, 2005.

INDEX